Data Structures and

Algorithms

An Easy Introduction

Author

Rudolph Russell

Table of Contents

CHAPTER 3 69

DEVELOPING EFFICIENT COMPUTER PROGRAMS....... 69

Chapter 1

Introduction to C++

C++ Programming Basics

If you want to build data structures and algorithms, you should realize that this requires communicating instructions to a computer. An excellent way to execute such communication is to use a high-level computer language, like C++.

C++ evolved from the programming language C, and has, over time, undergone further evolution and development from its original starting point. In C++, you'll find more features that aren't available in the C language, such as constants, in-line function substitution, reference types, parametric polymorphism through templates, and exceptions.

As a result, C++ has grown to become a complex programming language. Additionally, you do not need to know every single detail about C++ language to use it as efficiently as possible t.

In this section, we'll go on a quick tour of C++ and its features. However, it would be impossible to offer a complete presentation of the language, due to space constraints. As a reader, you should have a good knowledge of programming, even if other programming language, like C# or Python, since we don't offer detailed descriptions. In this part of this book you'll go through the basics of the language, and also get a closer look at the C++ language features. Next, we will focus on object-oriented programming concepts.

The C++ programming language is a very flexible language, based on C; we can call it "C with object oriented features" or "C with classes." Thus, with minor exceptions, C++ is a superset of the C programming language. C++ shares C's ability to deal efficiently with hardware at the level of bits, bytes, words, addresses, etc. In fact, this language adds many additional features over C (hence why it's named C++"), with the principal enhancement being the object-oriented concept of a *class*.

A class is a user-defined type that encapsulates many important mechanisms such as guaranteed initialization, implicit type conversion, control of memory management, operator overloading, and polymorphism (which are all important topics that will be discussed later in this book). A class also has the ability to hide its own underlying data.

This allows a class to conceal its implementation details ,and make it easy for the user to imagine the class concept as an interface.

The output of these programs is very easy to understand and, in order to deal with program maintenance, something called "a machine-code interpretation of this program" is created. **Another program,** Another concept, the linker (which is typically invoked automatically by the compiler), includes any necessary library code functions and produces the final machine-executable file. In order to run our program, the user requests that the system execute this file.

o illustrate some of the language's basic elements, we'll consider a very simple program. Don't worry if some of the elements in this example aren't fully explained.

We will discuss them in greater detail later in this chapter. This program inputs two integers, which are stored in the variables x and y. It then computes the sum, stores the result in a variable sum, and, finally, it outputs this sum.

(The line numbers aren't part of the program; they're here just for reference.)

```
1 #include <cstdlib>
2 #include <iostream>
3 /* This program inputs two numbers, x and y, and outputs
their sum, */
4 int main() {
5 int x, y;
6 std::cout << "Please enter two numbers: ";
7 std::cin >> x >> y; // input x and y
8 int sum = x + y; // compute their sum
9 std::cout << "Their sum is " << sum << std::endl;
```

10 return EXIT SUCCESS; // terminate successfully

11 }

A few things about this C++ program should be fairly obvious. First, comments are indicated with two slashes (//). Each such comment extends to the end of the line. Longer block comments are enclosed between /* and */. Block comments may extend over multiple lines. The quantities manipulated by this program are stored in three integer variables: x, y, and sum. The operators ">>" and "<<" are used for input and output, respectively.

Program Elements

Let's consider the elements of the above program in greater detail. Lines 1 and 2 input the two **header files**, "cstdlib" and "iostream." Header files are used to provide special information and definitions, which are useful to the program. The first provides standard system definitions, and the second provides the definitions needed for input and output. The initial entry point for C++ programs is the function main. The statement "int main( )" on line 4 declares "main" to be a function that **takes no arguments** and returns an integer result. (In general, the main function may be referred to by the command-line arguments, but we won't discuss this.)

The *function body* is given within braces, or curly brackets ({...}), that begin on line 4 and end on line 11. The program terminates when the return statement on line 10 is executed. By convention, the function main returns to the zero value to indicate success, and returns a nonzero value to indicate failure. They include the cstdlib file, which defines the constant EXIT SUCCESS to be 0. Thus, the return statement on line 10 returns 0, indicating a successful termination.

The statement on line 6 prints a string using the output operator ("<<"). The statement on line 7 inputs the values of the variables x and y using the input operator (">>"). These variable values could be supplied, for example, by the person running the program. The name std::cout indicates that output will be sent to the *standard output stream*.

There are two other important I/O streams in C++: *standard input* is where input is typically read, and *standard error* is where error output is written. These are denoted std::cin and std::cerr, respectively. The prefix "std::" indicates that these objects come from the system's **standard library**. We should use this prefix when we're referring to objects from the standard library.

Nevertheless, it's possible to inform the compiler that we wish to use objects from the standard library.

C++ Data Types

You'll find the following data types in the C++ programming language.

Bool: Boolean value, either true or false

Char: character

Short: short integer

Int: integer

Long: long integer

Float: single-precision floating-point number

Double: double-precision floating-point number

There is also an enumeration, or enum, type to represent a set of discrete values. Together, enumerations and the types bool, char, and int are called integral types. Finally, there is a special type, void, which explicitly indicates the absence of any type of information. Let's discuss each of these types in greater detail.

Characters

A char variable holds a single character. A char in C++ is typically 8-bits, but the exact number of bits used for a char variable depends on the specific implementation in question. By allowing different implementations to define the meaning of basic

types, such as char, C++ can tailor its generated code to each machine architecture

and, in doing so, achieve maximum efficiency. However, this flexibility can be a source of frustration for programmers who want to write machine-independent programs.

A literal is a constant value that appears in a program. Character literals are

enclosed in single quotes, as in 'a', 'Q', and '+'. A backslash (\) is used to

specify a number of special character literals as shown below.

'\n' newline

'\t' tab

'\b' backspace

'\0' null

'\'' single quote

'\"' double quote

'\\' backslash

The null character, '\0', is sometimes used to indicate the end of a string of characters. Every character is associated with an integer code. The function int(ch)

returns the integer value associated with a character variable, ch.

Integers

An int variable holds an integer. Integers come in three sizes: short int, (plain)

int, and long int. The terms "short" and "long" are synonyms for "short int" and

"long int," respectively. Decimal numbers such as 0, 25, 98765, and -3 are of type

int. The suffix "l" or "L" can be added to indicate a long integer, as in 123456789L.

Octal (base 8) constants are specified by prefixing the number with the zero digit, and hexadecimal (base 16) constants can be specified by prefixing the number with "0x." For example, the literals 256, 0400, and 0x100 all represent the integer value 256 (in decimal).

When declaring a variable, we have the option of providing a definition, or initial value. If no definition is given, the initial value is unpredictable, so each variable should have a value assigned to it before it can be used.

Variable names may consist of any combination of letters, digits, or the underscore (_) character, but the first character can't be a digit. Here are some examples of declarations of integral variables.

```
short n; // n's value is undefined

int octalNumber = 0400;

// 400 (base 8) = 256 (base 10)

char newline character = '\n';

long BIGnumber = 314159265L;

short aSTRANGE 1234 variABlE NaMe;
```

Although you can begin a variable name with an underscore, it's best to avoid doing so, since some C++ compilers use this convention for defining their own internal identifiers.

C++ doesn't specify the exact number of bits in each type, but a short is at least 16 bits long, and a long is at least 32 bits. Actually, you won't find any requirement that long be strictly longer than short. Given a type, TO, the expression size of(T) returns the size of type T, expressed as some **amount** of multiples of the size of char. For example, in typical systems, a char is 8 bits long, and an int is 32 bits long. Thus, the sizeof(int) is 4.

Enumerations

An enumeration is a user-defined type that can hold any of a set of discrete values.

Once defined, enumerations behave much like the integer type. A common use for enumerations is providing meaningful names to a set of related values. Each element of an enumeration is associated with an integer value. By default, these values count upwards from 0, but it's also possible to define explicit constant values as shown below.

```
enum Day { SUN, MON, TUE, WED, THU, FRI, SAT };

enum Mood { HAPPY = 3, SAD = 1, ANXIOUS = 4, SLEEPY = 2 };

Day today = THU; // today may be any of MON... SAT

Mood myMood = SLEEPY; // myMood may be HAPPY,..., SLEEPY
```

Since we didn't specify values, SUN would be associated with 0, MON with 1, and so on. As you can see, you must write the names of the enumeration and also the constants with all capital letters.

Basic C++ Programming Elements

Floating Point

A e float type variable holds a single-precision floating-point number, and a double type variable holds a double-precision floating-point number.C++ leaves the exact number of bits in each of the floating point types undefined, as it does with integers. By default, floating point literals, such as 3.14159 and -1234.567, are double type

f. Two types of notation are possible: e or E.

Pointers

Each program variable is stored in the computer's memory at a given location or address. A pointer is a variable that holds the value of such an address. Given a type T, the type T* denotes a pointer of a variable of type T. For example, int* denotes a pointer to an integer.

Two essential operators are used to manipulate pointers. The first returns the address of an object in memory, and the second returns the contents of a given address. In C++ the first task is performed by the address-of operator, &. For example if x is an integer variable in your program &x is the address of x in memory.

Accessing an object's value from its address is known as dereferencing. This is accomplished using the * operator. For example, if we were to declare q to be a pointer to an integer (that is, int*) and then set q = &x, we could access x's value with *q.

Assigning an integer value to *q effectively changes the value of x.

Consider, for example, the code fragment below. The variable p is declared to be a pointer to a char, and is initialized to point to the variable ch. Thus, *p is another way of referring to ch. You can observe that, when the value of ch changes, the value of *p changes as well.

```
char ch = 'Q';

char* p = &ch; // p holds the address of ch

cout << *p; // outputs the character 'Q'

ch = 'Z'; // ch now holds 'Z'

cout << *p; // outputs the character 'Z'

*p = 'X'; // ch now holds 'X'

cout << ch; // outputs the character 'X'
```

Arrays

An array is a collection of elements of the same type. Given any type T and a

constant N, a variable of type T[N] holds an array of N elements, each of type T.

Each element of the array is referenced by its index — that is, a number from 0 to N − 1. The following statements declare two arrays; one holds three doubles, and the other holds 10 double pointers.

```
double f[5]; // array of 5 doubles: f[0],..., f[4]

int m[10]; // array of 10 ints: m[0],..., m[9]

f[4] = 2.5;

m[2] = 4;

cout << f[m[2]]; // outputs f[4], which is 2.5
```

Constants and Typedef

Programmers like to associate names with constant quantities.

By adding the keyword "const" to a declaration, we can indicate that the value of the associated object can't be changed. Constants can be used virtually anywhere that literals can: for example, in an array declaration. To improve understanding, we'll use all capital letters when naming constants.

const double PI = 3.14159265;

const int CUT OFF[ ] = {90, 80, 70, 60};

const int N DAYS = 7;

const int N HOURS = 24*N DAYS; // using a constant expression

int counter[N HOURS]; // an array of 168 ints

Local and Global Scopes

When a group of C++ statements are enclosed in curly brackets ({...}), they define a block. Variables and types that are declared within a block are only accessible from within the block. They are said to be local to the block.

Blocks can be nested within other blocks. In C++, a variable may be defined as being external to every block.

Such a variable is global, in the sense that it can be accessed from everywhere in the program. The sections of a program from which a given name is accessible are known as its scope.

Namespaces

A namespace is a mechanism that allows a group of related names to be defined in one place. This helps organize global objects into natural groups and minimizes the problems of globals. For example, the following sequence identifies a namespace, myglobals, containing two variables, cat and dog.

namespace myglobals {

```
int cat;

string dog = "bow wow";

}
```

The Using Statement

If we are repeatedly using variables from the same namespace, it's possible to avoid entering namespace specifiers by telling the system that we want to "use" a particular specifier. We communicate this desire with the using statement, which makes some or all of the names from the namespace accessible, without explicitly providing the specifier. The purpose of this statement is to show users the two different methods of listing the names in any namespace.

```
using std::string; // makes just std::string accessible

using std::cout; // makes just std::cout accessible

using namespace myglobals; // makes all of myglobals accessible
```

Expressions

An expression combines variables and literals with operators to create new values.

In the following sequence, we'll group operators according to the types of objects they may be applied to. Throughout, we'll use var to denote a variable or anything to which a value may be assigned. (In official C++ jargon, this is called an lvalue.)

We use exp to denote an expression and type to denote a type.

Member Selection and Indexing

Arithmetic Operators

The following are the binary arithmetic operators:

exp + exp addition

exp − exp subtraction

exp * exp multiplication

exp / exp division

exp % exp modulo (remainder)

There are also unary minus (–x) and unary plus (+x) operations. Division between two integer operands results in an integer result by truncation.

Increment and Decrement Operators

The post-increment operator returns a variable's value and then increments it by 1. The post-decrement operator is analogous, but it decreases the value by 1 instead. The pre-increment operator first increments the variables, and then returns the value.

var ++ post increment

var −− post decrement

++ var pre increment

−− var pre decrement

The following code segment illustrates the increment and decrement operators.

int a[ ] = {0, 1, 2, 3};

int i = 2;

int j = i++; // j = 2 and now i = 3

int k = −−i; // now i = 2 and k = 2

cout << a[k++]; // a[2] (= 2) is output; now k = 3

Relational and Logical Operators

C++ provides the usual comparison operators.

exp < exp less than

exp > exp greater than

exp <= exp less than or equal

exp >= exp greater than or equal

exp == exp equal to

exp != exp not equal to

These return a Boolean result: either true or false. Comparisons can be made with these numbers or chars or strings without using C Style.

Pointers can also be compared, but generally it's only worth it to test whether pointers are equal or not equal (since their values are memory addresses).

The following logical operators are also given.

! exp logical not

exp && exp logical and

exp | | exp logical or

Bitwise Operators

These operators act on the representations of numbers as binary bit strings.

They can be applied to any integer type, and the result is an integer type.

˜ exp bitwise complement

exp & exp bitwise and

exp ^ exp bitwise exclusive-or

exp | exp bitwise or

exp1 << exp2 shift exp1 left by exp2 bits

exp1 >> exp2 shift exp1 right by exp2 bits

Assignment Operators

In addition to the familiar assignment operator (=), C++ includes a special form for each of the arithmetic binary operators (+, −, *, /, %) and each of the bitwise binary operators (&, |, ^, <<, >>), that combines a binary operation with an assignment. For example, the statement "n += 2" means "n = n + 2." Some examples are shown below.

int i = 10;

int j = 5;

string s = "yes";

i −= 4; // i = i - 4 = 6

j *= −2; // j = j * (-2) = -10

s += " or no"; // s = s + " or no" = "yes or no"

Control Flow

Control flow in C++ is similar to that of other high-level languages. In this section, we will review the basic structure and syntax of control flow in C++, including method returns, if statements, switch statements, loops, and restricted forms of "jumps" (the break and continue statements).

If Statement

Every programming language includes a way of making choices, and C++ is no exception. The most common method of making choices in a C++ program is through the use of an if statement. The syntax of an if statement in C++ is shown below, as is a small example.

if (condition)

true statement

else if (condition)

else if statement

else

else statement

Here is a simple

example.

```
if ( snowLevel < 2 ) {

goToClass(); // do this if snow level is less than 2

comeHome();

}

else if ( snowLevel < 5 )

haveSnowballFight(); // if level is at least 2 but less than 5

else if ( snowLevel < 10 )

goSkiing(); // if level is at least 5 but less than 10

else

stayAtHome(); // if snow level is 10 or more
```

Switch Statement

A switch statement provides an efficient way to distinguish between many different options, according to the value of an integral type. Observe the following example:

A char command:

```
cin >> command; // input command character

switch (command) { // switch based on command value

case 'I' : // if (command == 'I')

editInsert();

break;

case 'D' : // else if (command == 'D')

editDelete();

break;

case 'R' : // else if (command == 'R')

editReplace();

break;

default : // else
```

```cpp
cout << "Unrecognized command\n";

break;

}
```

While and Do-While Loops

C++ has two kinds of conditional loops for iterating over a set of statements, as long as some specified condition holds. These two loops are the standard, **while loop and the do-while loop**. One loop tests a Boolean condition before performing an iteration of the loop body, and the other tests a condition after the fact. Let's consider the while loop first.

```cpp
while ( condition )

loop body statement

int a[100];

//...

int i = 0;
```

```
int sum = 0;

while (i < 100 && a[i] >= 0) {

sum += a[i++];

}
```

For Loop

Many loops involve three common elements: an initialization, a condition under which to continue execution, and an increment to be performed after each execution of the loop's body. A for loop conveniently encapsulates these three elements.

```
for ( initialization ; condition ; increment )

loop body statement

const int NUM ELEMENTS = 100;

double b[NUM ELEMENTS];

//...
```

```cpp
for (int i = 0; i < NUM ELEMENTS; i++) {

if (b[i] > 0)

cout << b[i] << '\n';

}
```

Break and Continue Statements

C++ provides statements to change control flow, including break, continue,

and return statements.

```cpp
int a[100];

//...

int sum = 0;

for (int i = 0; i < 100; i++) {
```

```
if (a[i] < 0) break;

sum += a[i];

}
```

Functions

A function is a chunk of code that can be called on to perform a well-defined task, such as calculating the area of a rectangle, computing the weekly withholding tax for a company employee, or sorting a list of names in ascending order. In order to define a function, we need to provide the compiler with the following information:

Return type. This specifies the type of value or object that is returned by the function. For example, a function that computes the area of a rectangle might return a double type value. A function is not required to return a value. For example, it may simply produce an output or modify some data structure.

Function name. This indicates the name given to the function. Ideally, you should name a function in such a way that the user will understand what the function does.

Argument list. This serves as a list of placeholders for the values that will be passed into the function. The actual values will be provided when the function is invoked. For example, a function that computes the area of a polygon might take four double arguments: the x- and y-coordinates of the rectangle's lower left corner and the x- and y-coordinates of the rectangle's upper right corner. As you can see, the list of parameters contains many variables that can be separated using a comma in the brackets, where each entry consists of the name of the argument and its type. A function may have any number of arguments, and the argument list may even be empty.

Function body. This is a collection of C++ statements that define the actual computations to be performed by the function. This is enclosed within curly brackets. If the function returns a value, the body will typically end with a return statement, which specifies the final function value.

```
bool evenSum(int a[ ], int n); // function declaration
bool evenSum(int a[ ], int n) { // function definition
int sum = 0;
for (int i = 0; i < n; i++) // sum the array elements
sum += a[i];
return (sum % 2) == 0; // returns true if sum is even
}
```

Overloading and Inlining

This definition implements the concept of code. Many functions can be **named overloading, but they all do different things**.

Function overloading occurs when two or more functions are defined with the same name, but with different argument lists. Such definitions are useful in situations where we need two functions that have essentially the same purpose, but accomplish it with different types of arguments.

```
void print(int x) // print an integer

{ cout << x; }

void print(const Passenger& pass) { // print a Passenger

cout << pass.name << " " << pass.mealPref;

if (pass.isFreqFlyer)

cout << " " << pass.freqFlyerNo;

}
```

Operator Overloading

C++ also allows overloading of operators, such as +, *, +=, and <<. Unsurprisingly, such a definition is referred to as operator overloading. Suppose you'd like to write an equality test for two passenger objects. We can denote this in a natural way by overloading the == operator, as shown below.

```cpp
bool operator==(const Passenger& x, const Passenger& y) {

return x.name == y.name

&& x.mealPref == y.mealPref

&& x.isFreqFlyer == y.isFreqFlyer

&& x.freqFlyerNo == y.freqFlyerNo;

}
```

In-line Functions

Very short functions may be defined as being "inline." This is a note to the compiler stating that it should simply expand the function code in place, rather than using the system's call-return mechanism. As a rule of thumb, in-line functions are very short (at most a few lines) and shouldn't involve any loops or conditionals. Here is an example, which returns the minimum of two integers.

```cpp
inline int min(int x, int y) { return (x < y ? x : y); }
```

Classes

The concept of a class is fundamental to C++, since it provides a way to define new user-defined types, complete with associated functions and operators. By restricting access to certain members of a given class, it's possible to figure out the properties that are essential to a correctly using the class, e based on the details needed for implementation.

Classes are fundamental to programming methods that use an object-oriented approach.

```
class Counter { // a simple counter

public:

Counter(); // initialization

int getCount(); // get the current count

void increaseBy(int x); // add x to the count

private:

int count; // the counter's value
```

```
};
```

```
Counter::Counter()  // constructor

{ count = 0; }
```

```
int Counter::getCount()  // get current count

{ return count; }
```

```
void Counter::increaseBy(int x)  // add x to the count

{ count += x; }
```

Access Control

One important feature of classes is the notion of access control. Members may be declared public, which means that they are accessible from outside the class, or private, which means that they are accessible only from within the class.

(We will discuss two exceptions to this later: protected access and friend functions.) In the previous example, we couldn't directly access the private member count from outside the class definition.

```
Counter ctr;  // ctr is an instance of Counter
```

```
//...
```

cout << ctr.count << endl; // ILLEGAL - count is private

Constructors

The name of a constructor member's function is the same as the class, and it has no return

type. Because objects may be initialized in different ways, it's natural to define different constructors and rely on function overloading to determine which one will be called.

```
class Passenger {

private:

//...

public:

Passenger(); // default constructor
```

```cpp
Passenger(const string& nm, MealType mp, const string& ffn
= "NONE");

Passenger(const Passenger& pass); // copy constructor

//...

};
```

Destructors

A constructor is called when a class object comes into existence. A destructor is a member function that is automatically called when a class object ceases to exist.

If a class object comes into existence dynamically, using the new operator, the destructor will be called when this object is destroyed using the delete operator.

```cpp
class Vect { // a vector class

public:

Vect(int n); // constructor, given size
```

```cpp
~Vect(); // destructor

//... other public members omitted

private:

int* data; // an array holding the vector

int size; // number of array entries

};

Vect::Vect(int n) { // constructor

size = n;

data = new int[n]; // allocate array

}

Vect::~Vect() { // destructor

delete [] data; // free the allocated array

}
```

Classes and Memory Allocation

When a class performs memory allocation using the new
operator, care must be taken to avoid a number of common

programming errors. Earlier, we showed that failure to the storage, deallocating in the destructor of a class, **causes the output to be in memory** . A somewhat more insidious problem occurs when the classes that allocate memory fail to provide a copy constructor or an assignment operator. Consider the following example, using our Vect class.

Vect a(100); // a is a vector of size 100

Vect b = a; // initialize b from a (DANGER!)

Vect c; // c is a vector (default size 10)

c = a; // assign a to c (DANGER!)

The declaration of object a invokes the vector constructor, which allocates an array of 100 integers and a.data points to this array. The declaration "Vect b=a" initializes b from a. In this example, we didn't provide another constructor in Vect variable, so the software will use the default one, which will copy each member of a to b. In particular, it sets "b.data=a.data."

Notice that this doesn't copy the contents of the array; rather, it copies the pointer to the array's initial element. This default action is sometimes called a shallow copy.

The declaration of c invokes the constructor with a default argument value of 10, and as such allocates an array of 10 elements in the free store. Because we haven't provided an assignment operator, the statement "c=a" also executes a shallow copy of a to c. Only pointers are copied, not array contents. Worse yet, we've lost the pointer to c's original 10-element array, thus creating a memory leak.

Now, a, b, and c all have members that point to the same array in the free store. If the contents of the arrays of one of the three were to change, the other two would mysteriously change as well. Worse yet, if one of the three were to be deleted before the others (for example, if this variable was declared in a nested block), the destructor would delete the shared array.

When either of the other two **attempts to** by accessing the deleted array, the outputs will be catastrophic. In other words, there will be many problems in this kind of situation.

Fortunately, there is a simple fix for all of these problems. The problems arose because we allocated memory and we used the system's default copy constructor and assignment operator. If a class allocates memory, you should provide a copy constructor and assignment operator to allocate new memory for making copies. A copy constructor for a class, T, is typically declared to take a single argument, which is a constant reference to an object of the same class — that is, T(const T& t).

As you can see in the following example, it will copy every one of the data members from one class to the other while allocating memory for any dynamic members.

Vect::Vect(const Vect& a) { // copy constructor from a

size = a.size; // copy sizes

data = new int[size]; // allocate new array

for (int i = 0; i < size; i++) { // copy the vector contents

data[i] = a.data[i];

}

```
}
```

The assignment operator is handled by overloading the = operator, as shown in the next segment of code. The argument "a" plays the role of the object on the right side of the assignment operator. The assignment operator deletes the existing array storage, allocates a new array of the proper size, and copies elements into this new array. The if statement checks against the possibility of self-assignment.

(Sometimes, this occurs when different variables reference the same object.)

We perform this check by using the keyword "this". For any instance of a class object, "this" is defined to be the address of this instance. If this equals the address of a, then this is a case of self-assignment, and we ignore the operation. Otherwise, we deallocate the existing array, allocate a new array, and copy the contents over.

```
Vect& Vect::operator=(const Vect& a) { // assignment
operator from a
```

```
if (this != &a) { // avoid self-assignment

delete [ ] data; // delete old array

size = a.size; // set new size

data = new int[size]; // allocate new array

for (int i=0; i < size; i++) { // copy the vector contents

data[i] = a.data[i];

}

}

return *this;

}
```

Class Friends and Class Members

These complicated data structures will interact with many different classes.

In this case, issues regarding the coordination of the tasks of these classes, to allow sharing of information, often develop. We'll discuss some of these issues in this section.

Earlier we said that private members of a class can only be accessed from within the class, but there is an exception. More specifically, we can declare a function to be a friend, which means that it may access the class's private data.

There are a number of reasons for defining friend functions. One is that syntax requirements might forbid you from defining a member function. For example, consider a class, SomeClass. Suppose that we want to define an overloaded output operator for this class, and that this output operator needs access to private member data. The class declares that the output operator is a friend of the class as shown below.

```
class SomeClass {

private:

int secret;

public:

//... // give << operator access to secret

friend ostream& operator<<(ostream& out, const
SomeClass& x);
```

```cpp
};

ostream& operator<<(ostream& out, const SomeClass& x)

{ cout << x.secret; }
```

Questions

1. Write an algorithm explaining a function to find the smallest and largest numbers in an array of integers ,and compare it to a C++ function that would do the same thing

2. What are the contents of string s after the following statements have been executed?

string s = "abc";

string t = "cde";

s += s + t[1] + s;

3. Write a short C++ function that takes an integer, n, and returns the sum of all the integers smaller than n.

4. Implement a class which has three variables of string, int, and float, that will represent the name of the

anything such as names of flowers, their numbers of petals, and their prices. Your class must include a constructor method that initializes each variable to an appropriate value, and your class should include functions for setting the value of each type and obtaining the value of each type.

Chapter 2

Introduction to Object Oriented Design

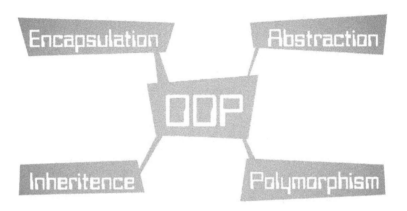

Abstraction

The notion of abstraction is that of distilling a complicated system down to its most fundamental components and describing these parts in simple, precise language. Typically, describing the parts of a system involves naming them and explaining their functionality. Applying the concept of abstraction to the design of data structures gives rise to abstract data types.

Encapsulation

Another important principle of object-oriented design is the concept of encapsulation, which states that different components of a software system shouldn't reveal the internal details of their respective implementations. One of the main advantages of encapsulation is that it gives the programmer freedom in implementing the details of a system. The only constraint for the programmer is maintaining the abstract interface that outsiders see.

Modularity

In addition to abstraction and encapsulation, a fundamental principle of object-oriented design is modularity. Modern software systems typically consist of several different components that must interact properly in order for the entire system to work properly. Keeping these interactions functioning correctly requires that these disparate components be well-organized. In object-oriented design, this code-structuring approach is centered on the concept of modularity. Modularity refers to an organizing principle for code, in which different components of a software system are divided into separate functional units

Inheritance and Polymorphism

Inheritance in C++

The object-oriented paradigm provides a modular and hierarchical organizational structure for reusing code through a technique called inheritance. This technique allows for the design of generic classes that can be specialized into particular classes, with the specialized classes reusing the code from the generic class. For example, suppose that we were designing a set of classes to represent the people at a university. We might have a generic class "Person," which defines elements common to all people.

We could then define specialized classes such as Student, Administrator, and Instructor, each of which provides specific information about a particular type of Person.

A generic class is also known as a base class, parent class, or superclass.

It defines "generic" members that apply in a multitude of situations. Any class that specializes or extends a base class need not give new implementations for the general functions, since it inherits them. It should only define those functions that are specialized for this particular class. Such a class is called a derived class, child class, or subclass.

Let's use an example to illustrate these concepts. Suppose that we were writing a program to deal with the people at a university. Below, we'll show a partial implementation of a generic class for a person. We use "//..." to indicate code that is irrelevant to this example and which, as such, has been omitted.

```
class Person { // Person (base class)

private:

string name; // name

string idNum; // university ID number

public:

//...
```

```cpp
void print(); // print information

string getName(); // retrieve name

};

class Student : public Person { // Student (derived from Person)

private:

string major; // major subject

int gradYear; // graduation year

public:

//...

void print(); // print information

void changeMajor(const string& newMajor); // change major

};
```

Member Functions

An object belonging to the type Person can access the public members of Person. An object of type Student can access the public members of both classes. If a Student object invokes the shared print function, it will use its own version by default. We use the class scope operator (::) to specify which class's function is used, as in Person::print and Student::print. Note that an object of type Person cannot access members of the base type, and thus it's impossible for a Person object to invoke the changeMajor function of class Student.

```
Person person("Mary", "12-345"); // declare a Person

Student student("Bob", "98-764", "Math", 2012); // declare a
Student

cout << student.getName() << endl; // invokes
Person::getName()

person.print(); // invokes Person::print()

student.print(); // invokes Student::print()
```

```
person.changeMajor("Physics"); // ERROR!

student.changeMajor("English"); // okay
```

Protected Members

Even though the class Student is inherited from the class Person, member functions of Student do not have access to private members of Person. For example, the following sequence would be illegal.

```
void Student::printName() {

cout << name << '\n'; // ERROR! name is private to Person

}
```

Polymorphism

"Polymorphism" literally means "many forms." In the context of object-oriented design, it refers to the ability of a variable to take on different types. Polymorphism is typically applied in C++ using pointer variables. In particular, if a variable, p, is declared to be a pointer to some class IS, this implies that p can point to any object belonging to any derived class T of S.

Interfaces and Abstract Classes

For two objects to interact, they must "know" about each other's member functions. To enforce this "knowledge," the object-oriented design paradigm asks that classes specify the application programming interface (API), or interface, that their objects present to other objects. In the ADT-based approach:

```
class Stack { // informal interface – not a class

public:

bool isEmpty() const; // is the stack empty?

void push(int x); // push x onto the stack

int pop(); // pop the stack and return result

};
```

Templates

Let's consider the following function, which returns the minimum of two integers.

int integerMin(int a, int b) // returns the minimum of a and b

{ return (a < b ? a : b); }

This kind of function is very useful, so we might want to define a similar function for computing the minimum of two variables of other types, such as long, short, float, and double. Each such function would require a different declaration and definition, however, and making many copies of the same function is a foolproof solution, especially for longer functions.

C++ provides an automatic mechanism, called the function template, to produce a generic function for an arbitrary type, T. A function template provides a well-defined pattern, from which a concrete function may later be formally defined or instantiated. The example below defines a genericMin function template.

```
template <typename T>
T genericMin(T a, T b) { // returns the minimum of a and b
return (a < b ? a : b);
}
```

The declaration takes the form of the keyword "template," followed by the notation <typename T>, which is the parameter list for the template, just one parameter T. The keyword "typename" indicates that T is the name of

some type. (Older versions of C++ do not support this keyword and instead the keyword "class" must be used.) We can have other types of template parameters — integers, for example — but type names are the most common. Note that the type parameter T takes the place of "int" in the original definition of the genericMin function.

We can now invoke our templated function to compute the minimum of objects of various types. The compiler looks at the argument types and determines which form of the function must be instantiated.

```
cout << genericMin(3, 4) << ' ' // = genericMin<int>(3,4)

<< genericMin(1.1, 3.1) << ' ' // =
genericMin<double>(1.1, 3.1)

<< genericMin('t', 'g') << endl; // =
genericMin<char>('t','g')
```

Exceptions

Exceptions are unexpected events that occur during the execution of a program. An exception may be the result of an error condition or simply an unanticipated input.

In C++, exceptions can be thought of as being objects themselves.

In C++, an exception is "thrown" by code that encounters an unexpected condition. Exceptions can also be thrown by the C++ runtime environment, should it encounter an unexpected condition like the possibility that it runs out of memory. A thrown exception is "caught" by other code that "handles" the exception somehow, or the program is terminated unexpectedly.

```cpp
class MathException { // generic math exception
public:
MathException(const string& err) // constructor
: errMsg(err) { }
string getError() { return errMsg; } // access error message
private:
string errMsg; // error message
};
try {
//... application computations
if (divisor == 0) // attempt to divide by 0?
```

```cpp
    throw ZeroDivide("Divide by zero in Module X");

}

catch (ZeroDivide& zde) {

// handle division by zero

}

catch (MathException& me) {

// handle any math exception other than division by zero

}
```

Questions

1. Explain some of the potential disadvantages of the inheritance trees--that is, a large set of classes, A, B, C, and so on, such that B extends A, C extends B, D extends C, etc.--with regard to efficiency.

2. Describe the disadvantages of shallow inheritance trees, which refers to, a large set of classes, A, B, C, and so on, such that all of these classes extend a single class, Z.

3. Write a class diagram for the following classes.
    1. Class Goat inherit Object and adds a member variable tail and Functions milk and jump.
    2. Class Pig extends Object and adds a member variable nose and Functions eat and wallow.

3. Class Horse extends Object and adds member variables height and color, and Functions run and jump.

4. Another class called Racer that inherits Horse and adds a Function, race.

5. Class Equestrian extends Horse and adds a member variable weight and the functions trot and isTrained

Chapter 3

Developing efficient computer programs

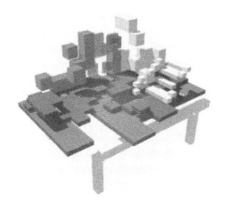

Arrays

Now we'll design a class, called Scores, to store information about our game scores. We store the highest scores in an array, entries. The maximum number of scores may vary from instance to instance, so we will create a member variable, maxEntries, that stores the desired maximum. Its value is specified when a Scores object is first constructed. In order to keep track of the actual number of entries, we define a member variable, numEntries.

It is initialized to zero, and it will be updated as entries are added or removed. We provide a constructor, a destructor, a member function for adding a new score, and another one for removing a score at a given index.

The definition is given in Code Fragment 3.3.

```
class Scores { // stores game high scores
public:
Scores(int maxEnt = 10); // constructor
~Scores(); // destructor
void add(const GameEntry& e); // add a game entry
GameEntry remove(int i) // remove the ith entry
throw(IndexOutOfBounds);
private:
int maxEntries; // maximum number of entries
int numEntries; // actual number of entries
GameEntry* entries; // array of game entries
```

};

The Code Fragment 3.3: A C++ class for storing high game scores.

In Code Fragment 3.4, we present the class constructor, which allocates the desired amount of storage for the array using the "new" operator. Recall from this section that C++ represents a dynamic array as a pointer to its first element, and this command returns such a pointer. The class destructor ~Scores deletes this array.

```
Scores::Scores(int maxEnt) { // constructor

maxEntries = maxEnt; // save the max size

entries = new GameEntry[maxEntries]; // allocate array storage

numEntries = 0; // initially no elements

}

Scores::~Scores() { // destructor
```

```
    delete[ ] entries;

}
```

Code Fragment 3.4: A C++ class GameEntry, representing a game entry.

The entries that have been added to the array are stored in indices 0 through numEntries −1. As more users play our video game, additional GameEntry objects are copied into the array. This is accomplished using the class's "add member function," which is described below. Only the highest maxEntries scores are retained. We also provide a member function, remove(i), which removes the entry at index i from

the array. We assume that $0 \leq i \leq numEntries - 1$. If not, the remove function throws an IndexOutOfBounds exception. We do not define this exception here, but it's derived from the class RuntimeException from the last section.

In our design, we have chosen to order the GameEntry objects by their score values, from highest to lowest. (In Exercise C-3.2, we explore an alternative design in which entries aren't ordered.) We illustrate an example of the data structure in

Mike	Rob	Paul	Anna	Rose	Jack				
1105	750	720	660	590	510				
0	1	2	3	4	5	6	7	8	9

Insertion

Next, let's consider how to add a new GameEntry e to the array of high scores. In particular, let's consider how we might perform the following update operation on an instance of the Scores class.

add(e): Insert game entry e into the collection of high scores. If this causes the number of entries to exceed maxEntries, the smallest is removed.

.

void Scores::add(const GameEntry& e) { // add a game entry

int newScore = e.getScore(); // score to add

if (numEntries == maxEntries) { // the array is full

```
if (newScore <= entries[maxEntries−1].getScore())

return; // not high enough - ignore

}

else numEntries++; // if not full, one more entry

int i = numEntries−2; // start with the next to last

while ( i >= 0 && newScore > entries[i].getScore() ) {

entries[i+1] = entries[i]; // shift right if smaller

i−−;

} e

ntries[i+1] = e; // put e in the empty spot

}
```

Sorting an Array

Algorithm InsertionSort(A):

Input: one array "A" of n numbers of elements

Output: this array "A" containing the elements that arranged in non-decreasing order for i ← 1 to n−1 do

{Insert A[i] at its proper location in A[0],A[1],...,A[i−1]}

cur ← A[i]

j ← i−1

while j ≥ 0 and A[j] > cur do

A[j + 1] ← A[j]

j ← j−1

A[j + 1] ← cur {cur is now in the right place}

void insertionSort(char* A, int n) { // sort an array of n characters

for (int i = 1; i < n; i++) { // insertion loop

char cur = A[i]; // current character to insert

int j = i − 1; // start at the previous character

while ((j >= 0) && (A[j] > cur)) { // while A[j] is out of order

A[j + 1] = A[j]; // move A[j] right

j--; // decrement j

}

A[j + 1] = cur; // this is the proper position for cur

}

Linked Lists

To explain it simply, linked lists are collections of nodes that together form a linear order. As in the children's game "Follow the Leader," each node stores a pointer.

class StringNode { // a node in a list of strings

private:

string elem; // element value

StringNode* next; // next item in the list

```cpp
friend class StringLinkedList; // provide StringLinkedList access

};

class StringLinkedList { // a linked list of strings
public:
StringLinkedList(); // empty list constructor
~StringLinkedList(); // destructor
bool empty() const; // is list empty?
const string& front() const; // get front element
void addFront(const string& e); // add to front of list
void removeFront(); // remove front item list
private:
StringNode* head; // pointer to the head of the list
};

StringLinkedList::StringLinkedList() // constructor
: head(NULL) { }
```

StringLinkedList::~StringLinkedList() // destructor

{ while (!empty()) removeFront(); }

bool StringLinkedList::empty() const // is list empty?

{ return head == NULL; }

const string& StringLinkedList::front() const // get front element

{ return head->elem; }

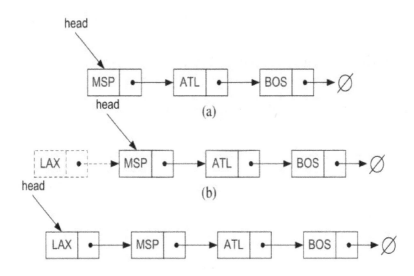

void StringLinkedList::addFront(const string& e) { // add to front of list

StringNode* v = new StringNode; // create new node

v−>elem = e; // store data

v−>next = head; // head now follows v

head = v; // v is now the head

}

Analysis of Algorithms

In general, each basic step in a pseudo-code description or a high-level language implementation corresponds to a small number of primitive operations (except for function calls, of course). Thus, we can perform a simple analysis of an algorithm, written in pseudo-code — which estimates the number of primitive operations executed up to a constant factor — by pseudo-code steps (but we must be careful, since, in some cases, a single line of pseudo-code may denote a number of steps).

Algorithm arrayMax(A,n):

Input: An array A storing n ≥ 1 integers.

Output: The maximum element in A.

currMax ← A[0]

for i ← 1 to n−1 do

if currMax < A[i] then

currMax ← A[i]

return currMax

The "Big-Oh" Notation

Let $f(n)$ and $g(n)$ be functions mapping non-negative integers to real numbers. We can say that $f(n)$ is $O(g(n))$ if there is a real constant $c > 0$ and an integer constant $n0 \geq 1$, such that $f(n) \leq cg(n)$, for $n \geq n0$.

Stacks

The concept of stacks is resembles a box of objects that are inserted and removed, according to the rule of last-in, first-out (LIFO).

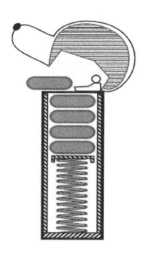

Stacks are the simplest of all data structures, yet they are also among the most important, since they are used in a host of different applications that include many more sophisticated data structures. Formally, a stack is an abstract data type (ADT) that supports the following operations:

push(e): Insert element e at the top of the stack.

pop(): Remove the top element from the stack; an error occurs

if the stack is empty.

top(): Return a reference to the top element of the stack, without removing it; an error occurs if the stack is empty.

In addition to these , we will also define the following functions:

size(): calling this function will return a number of elements in your stack

#include <stack>

using std::stack; // make stack accessible

stack<int> myStack; // a stack of integers

size(): This function will return a number of the elements in the box "stack".

empty(): Using this method will return a "true" if the stack is empty and "false" if not.

push(e): Push e onto the top of the stack.

pop(): Pop the element at the top of the stack.

top(): Return a reference to the element at the top of the stack.

template <typename E>

class ArrayStack {

```cpp
enum { DEF CAPACITY = 100 }; // default stack capacity

public:

ArrayStack(int cap = DEF CAPACITY); // constructor
from capacity

int size() const; // number of items in the stack

bool empty() const; // is the stack empty?

const E& top() const throw(StackEmpty); // get the top
element

void push(const E& e) throw(StackFull); // push the
element onto stack

void pop() throw(StackEmpty); // pop the stack

//...housekeeping functions omitted

private: // member data

E* S; // array of stack elements

int capacity; // stack capacity

int t; // index of the top of the stack

};
```

Queues

A queue is a close relative of the stack. A queue is a container of elements that are inserted and removed according to the first-in first-out (FIFO) principle.

The abstract data type (ADT) queue supports the following operations:

enqueue(e): Insert element e at the rear of the queue.

dequeue(): Remove element at the front of the queue; an error occurs

if the queue is empty.

front(): Return, but do not remove, a reference to the front element in the queue; an error occurs if the queue is empty.

The ADT queue also includes the following supporting member functions:

size(): Return the number of elements in the queue.

empty(): The return is true if the queue is empty, and false otherwise.

Trees

A tree is simply an abstract data type that stores many elements hierarchically. With the exception of the top element, each element in a tree has a parent element and zero or more child elements. A tree is usually represented visually by placing elements inside ovals or rectangles, and by using straight lines to illustrate the connections between parents and children. We typically call the top element the root of the tree, but it's as the highest element, with the other elements connected beneath it (just the opposite of a botanical tree).

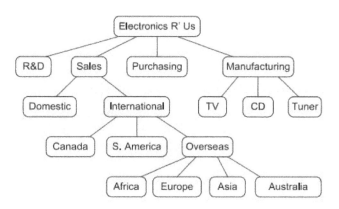

```cpp
template <typename E> // base element type
class Position<E> { //  position of a node
public:
E& operator*(); // get element
Position parent() const; // get parent
PositionList children() const; // get the  children of a node
bool isRoot() const; // root node?
bool isExternal() const; // external node?
};


template <typename E> // base element type
class Tree<E> {
public: // public types
class Position; //  position of a node
```

```
class PositionList; // a list of positions

public: // public functions

int size() const; // number of nodes

bool empty() const; // is the tree empty?

Position root() const; // get the root

PositionList positions() const; // get positions of all nodes

};
```

Binary Trees

A binary tree is an ordered tree in which every node has at most two children.

1. Every node has at most two children.

2. Each child node is labeled as being either a left child or a right child.

3. The left child precedes the right child in the ordering of children of the node.

```cpp
template <typename E> // base element type

class Position<E> { // a node position

public:

E& operator*(); // get element

Position left() const; // get left child

Position right() const; // get right child

Position parent() const; // get parent

bool isRoot() const; // root of tree?

bool isExternal() const; // an external node?

};
```

Hash Table

```cpp
template <typename K, typename V, typename H>

class HashMap {

public: // public types

typedef Entry<const K,V> Entry; // a (key,value) pair
```

```cpp
class Iterator; // an iterator/position

public: // public functions

HashMap(int capacity = 100); // constructor

int size() const; // number of entries

bool empty() const; // is the map empty?

Iterator find(const K& k); // find entry with a key, k

Iterator put(const K& k, const V& v); // insert/replace (k,v)

void erase(const K& k); // remove entry with key k

void erase(const Iterator& p); // erase entry at p

Iterator begin(); // iterator to first entry

Iterator end(); // iterator to end entry

protected: // protected types

typedef std::list<Entry> Bucket; // a bucket of entries

typedef std::vector<Bucket> BktArray; // a bucket array

//...insert HashMap utilities here

private:
```

```
int n; // number of entries

H hash; // the hash comparator

BktArray B; // bucket array

public: // public types

//...insert Iterator class declaration here

};
```

Sorting algorithms

Divide-and-Conquer

The Merge-sort is just an algorithm based on a design pattern called "divide-and-conquer".

The divide-and-conquer pattern consists of the next three steps:

1. Divide: If the input size does not attain a certain threshold (say, one or two elements), solve the problem directly with a

straightforward method and return the solution that was obtained. Otherwise, divide the input data into two or more disjoint subsets.

2. Recur: Recursively solve the sub-problems associated with the subsets.

3. Conquer: Take the solutions to the sub-problems and "merge" them into a solution to the original problem.

```
template <typename E, typename C> // merge-sort S
void mergeSort(list<E>& S, const C& less) {
typedef typename list<E>::iterator Itor; // sequence of elements
int n = S.size();
if (n <= 1) return; // already sorted
list<E> S1, S2;
Itor p = S.begin();
for (int i = 0; i < n/2; i++) S1.push back(*p++); // copy first half to S1
```

```cpp
for (int i = n/2; i < n; i++) S2.push back(*p++); // copy
second half to S2

S.clear(); // clear S's contents

mergeSort(S1, less); // recur on first half

mergeSort(S2, less); // recur on second half

merge(S1, S2, S, less); // merge S1 and S2 into S
}

template <typename E, typename C> // merge utility
void merge(list<E>& S1, list<E>& S2, list<E>& S, const
C& less) {

typedef typename list<E>::iterator Itor; // sequence of
elements

Itor p1 = S1.begin();

Itor p2 = S2.begin();

while(p1 != S1.end() && p2 != S2.end()) { // until either is
empty

if(less(*p1, *p2)) // append smaller to S
```

```
S.push back(*p1++);

else

S.push back(*p2++);

} w

hile(p1 != S1.end()) // copy rest of S1 to S

S.push back(*p1++);

while(p2 != S2.end()) // copy rest of S2 to S

S.push back(*p2++);

}
```

Quick-Sort

Like merge-sort, this algorithm is also based on the divide-and-conquer paradigm, but it uses this technique in a somewhat contrasting manner, as all the hard work has already been done before the recursive calls.

1. Divide: If S has at least two elements (nothing needs to be done if S has

zero or one element), select a specific element, x, from S, which is called the pivot. As is common practice, choose the pivot, x, to be the last element in S. Remove all the elements from S and put them into three sequences:

• L, storing the elements in S less than x.

• E, to store the elements in "S" == " x".

• G, storing the elements in S greater than x.

Of course, if the elements of S are all distinct, then E holds just one element:

1. the pivot itself.

2. Recur: Recursively sort sequences L and G.

3. Conquer: Put the elements back into S in order by first inserting the elements of L, then those of E, and finally those of G.

Questions

1. What is the best way to multiply a chain of matrices with dimensions "10×5, 5×2, 2×20, 20×12, 12×4, and 4×60"? Explain your work.

2. Develop an efficient algorithm for the matrix-chain multiplication problem, which outputs a fully parenthesized expression, for how to multiply the matrices in the chain using the minimum number of operations.